How To Organize A Speech In Order To Make Your Point

How to put together a speech that will capture and hold your audience's attention

"Practical, proven techniques that will help you to make your next speech a success"

Dr. Jim Anderson

Published by:
Blue Elephant Consulting
Tampa, Florida

Printed in the United States of America

Library of Congress Control Number: 2016920286

ISBN-13:   978-1540855046
ISBN-10:   154085504X

Warning – Disclaimer

Recent Books By The Author

Product Management

- Managing Your Product Manager Career: How Product Managers Can Find And Succeed In The Right Job

- How Product Managers Can Sell More Of Their Product: Tips & Techniques For Product Managers To Better Understand How To Sell Their Product

- Product Development Lessons For Product Managers: How Product Managers Can Create Successful Products

Public Speaking

- Changing How You Speak To Overcome Your Fear Of Speaking: Change techniques that will transform a speech into a memorable event

- Delivering Excellence: How To Give Presentations That Make A Difference: Presentation techniques that will transform a speech into a memorable event

CIO Skills

- Keeping The Barbarians Out: How CIOs Can Secure Their Department and Company: Tips And Techniques For CIOs To Use In Order To Secure Both Their IT

Department And Their Company

- What CIOs Need To Know In Order To Successfully Manage An IT Department: Decision Making Skills That Every CIO Needs To Have In Order To Be Able To Make The Right Choices

- How CIOs Can Make Innovation Happen: Tips And Techniques For CIOs To Use In Order To Make Innovation Happen In Their IT Department

IT Manager Skills

- How To Build High Performance IT Teams: Tips And Techniques That IT Managers Can Use In Order To Develop Productive Teams

- Building The Perfect Team: What Staffing Skills Do IT Managers Need?: Tips And Techniques That IT Managers Can Use In Order To Correctly Staff Their Teams

- Secrets Of Effective Leadership For IT Managers: Tips And Techniques That IT Managers Can Use In Order To Develop Leadership Skills

Negotiating

- Exploring How To Get The Deal That You Want In A Negotiation: How To Develop The Skill Of Exploring What Is Possible In A Negotiation In Order To Reach The

Best Possible Deal

- Use The Power Of Arguing To Win Your Next Negotiation: How To Develop The Skill Of Effective Arguing In A Negotiation In Order To Get The Best Possible Outcome

Miscellaneous

- How To Heal A Broken Leg – Fast!: Understanding how to deal with a broken leg in order to start walking again quickly

- How Software Defined Networking (SDN) Is Going To Change Your World Forever: The Revolution In Network Design And How It Affects

Note: See a complete list of books by Dr. Jim Anderson at the back of this book.

Acknowledgements

Any book like this one is the result of years of real-world work experience. In my over 25 years of working for 7 different firms, I have met countless fantastic people and I've been mentored by some truly exceptional ones. Although I've probably forgotten some of the people who made me the person that I am today, here is my attempt to finally give them the recognition that they so truly deserve:

- Thomas P. Anderson
- Art Puett
- Bobbi Marshall
- Bob Boggs

Dr. **Jim** Anderson

This book is dedicated to my family: Lori, Maddie, Nick, and Ben. None of this would have been possible without their constant love and support.

Thanks for always believing in me and providing me with the strength to always be willing to go out there and be my best for you.

Speaking.   Negotiating.   Managing.   Marketing.

Table of Contents

Organization Is The Key To Making Your Point

The first step in creating a speech that will allow you to make your point is to first determine how best to organize it. There are a lot of different ways to go about doing this, but you are going to want to make sure that you'll be able to connect with your audience. This means that you'll need to be able to determine what your emotional intelligence quotient is.

If we want to make sure that we've organized our thoughts in a way that will allow us to get our message across to our audience, it can be helpful to look for guidance from those who have done it well in the past. One fantastic example is Nelson Mandel who really knew how to customize a speech.

Where you'll be speaking will play a role in how your audience interprets your speech. If you know how to use a room, then you and your message will be well received. In order to make this happen, you are going to have to employ your room IQ.

When we agree to give a speech, we hope that we can provide our audience with an uplifting message. However, there are times that we are called on to deliver bad news. We still have an obligation to connect with our audience and we need to make sure that the bad news does not obscure the importance of our message.

Organizing a speech involves more than just getting your introduction correct, you also have to manage your message. If you have been asked to apologize for something, how you structure your speech is going to be critical.

Every speech that we give occupies a set amount of time. The time that we have allocated and the time that we use may be two different things. As speakers, we need to make sure that we fully understand the power of time and that we use it to our best advantage during our next speech.

For more information on what it takes to be a great public speaker, check out my blog, The Accidental Communicator, at:

www.TheAccidentalCommunicator.com

Good luck!

       - Dr. Jim Anderson

About The Author

I must confess that I never set out to be a public speaker. When I went to school, I studied Computer Science and thought that I'd get a nice job programming and that would be that. Well, at least part of that plan worked out!

My first job was working for Boeing on their F/A-18 fighter jet program. I spent my days programming fighter jet software in assembly language and I loved it. The U.S. government decided to save some money and went looking for other countries to sell this plane to. This put me into an unfamiliar role: I started to meet with foreign military officials and I ended up having to give speeches in order to explain what my product did.

Time moved on and so did I. I found myself working for Siemens, the big German telecommunications company. They were making phone switches and selling them to the seven U.S. phone companies. The problem was that the switches were too complicated. Customers couldn't tell the difference between one complicated phone switch from another complicated phone switch. Once again I found myself standing in front of the room giving speeches in order to explain what these complicated machines did and why ours were better than anyone else's.

I've spent over 25 years working as a product manager for both big companies and startups. This has given me an opportunity to do many, many presentations for customers, at conferences, and everywhere in-between.

I now live in Tampa Florida where I spend my time managing my consulting business, Blue Elephant Consulting, teaching college courses at the University of South Florida, and traveling to work with companies like yours to share the knowledge that I have about how to create and deliver powerful and effective speeches.

I'm always available to answer questions and I can be reached at:

Dr. Jim Anderson

Blue Elephant Consulting

Email: jim@BlueElephantConsulting.com

Facebook: http://goo.gl/1TVoK

Web: **www.BlueElephantConsulting.com**

"Unforgettable communication skills that will set your ideas free..."

Create Speeches That Motivate Your Audiences And Get Your Message Heard!

Dr. Jim Anderson is available to provide training and coaching on the topics that are the most important to people who have to speak in public: how can I create a speech that people want to hear and how can I deliver in a way that will allow me to connect with my audience and get my point across to them?

Dr. Anderson believes that in order to both learn and remember what he says, speakers need to laugh. Each one of his speeches is full of fun and humor so that what he says "sticks" with everyone.

Dr. Anderson's Public Speaking Training Includes:

1. How to plan your next speech: pick your purpose and understand your audience.
2. What's the best way to get PowerPoint and Keynote to work with you, not against you?
3. What do you need to do when you are presenting in order to truly connect with your audience?

Dr. Jim Anderson presents over 100 speeches per year. To invite Dr. Anderson to speak at your event, contact him at:

Phone: 813-418-6970 or
Email: jim@BlueElephantConsulting.com

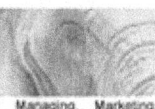

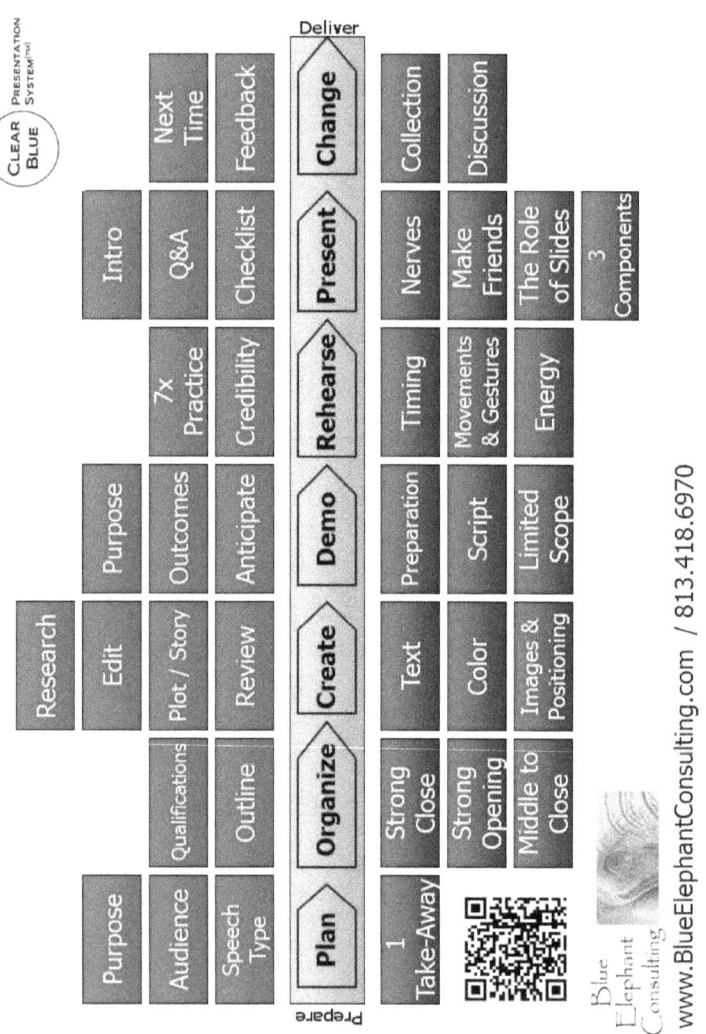

Blue Elephant Consulting has created the **Clear Blue™ Presentation System** for creating and delivering powerful and memorable presentations. The contents of this book are based on lessons learned during the development of the Clear Blue system. Contact Blue Elephant Consulting to learn more about the Clear Blue presentation system.

Chapter 1

Speakers Need To Know What Their Emotional Intelligence Quotient Is

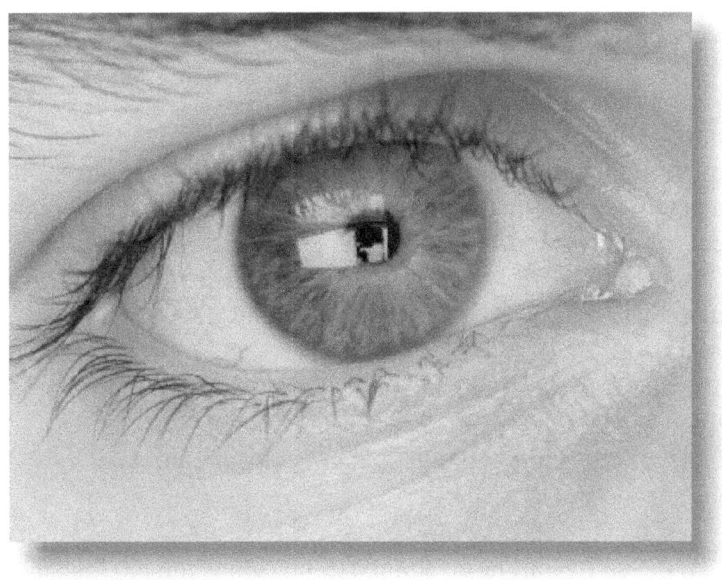

Chapter 1: Speakers Need To Know What Their Emotional Intelligence Quotient Is

Have you ever been giving a speech when all of a sudden you thought to yourself **"I wonder what they are thinking?"** I mean, you're standing up there running your mouth and the audience is sitting out there looking at you, but do you really know what's running through their heads right then? If you did know, how would that change what you were saying? It turns out that the best speakers DO know what their audience is thinking and they DO adjust their speeches to match this. You can do it also – you just need to have emotional intelligence...

What Is Emotional Intelligence?

So I'm sure that we all at least think that we know what **emotional intelligence** is, but do we really know? From a top-level view, emotional intelligence is simply the speaker's ability to be aware of their own emotions and the emotions of those who are around them.

It turns out that emotional intelligence is very important in our overall success. Somewhat surprisingly, studies have shown that a person's emotional intelligence can be **a bigger factor** in their overall success than their intellectual aptitude. In fact, some say that up to 90% of the success that you'll have in your life can be directly tied back to your emotional intelligence.

The author Daniel Goleman who wrote the book Emotional Intelligence: Why It Can Matter More Than IQ believes that there are **four "pillars"** to your emotional intelligence:

- **Self-awareness:** understanding what you are feeling at any point in time

- **Self-management of behaviors:** the ability to control your emotions including your body language, facial expressions, etc.

- **Social Awareness:** the ability to be aware of what people around you are feeling.

- **Relationship Management:** the ability to develop and foster relationships with others.

The good news about emotional intelligence is that these types of skills can be **taught and learned**. One of the key skills is for you as a speaker to become adept at reading facial expressions.

As a speaker, in order to truly connect with your audience you are going to want to **create the correct mood between you and your audience**. This means that you are going to have to be able to identify what their current energy level is so that you'll know how to steer it going forward. Based on your opening comments, you should be able to read your audience's facial expressions and using your emotional intelligence you should be able to determine what their mood is.

This ability to **"read" your audience** and adapt to their mood is what can turn a good speech into a great speech. Audiences really respond to a speaker who seems to fully understand where they are at. If you can use your emotional intelligence to connect with your audience, then you will be well on your way to becoming a great speaker.

What Does All Of This Mean For You?

The goal of any speaker is to find a way to **connect with their audience** while they are delivering a speech. A powerful tool that we have to do this is called our emotional intelligence. This skill is simply our ability to be aware of how we are currently feeling and how our audience is feeling.

Once we are aware of the power of our emotional intelligence and know how to use it, **we can change how we give speeches**. Being able to sense how our audience is feeling gives us the ability to adjust how we deliver a speech on the fly. We can adapt our message to how our audience is currently feeling.

Speakers who are able to connect with their audience **are the most powerful**. They have the ability to change the world just a little bit with each speech that they give. Use your emotional intelligence to connect with your audience and watch what happens!

Chapter 2

Nelson Mandela's Tips On How To Customize Your Next Speech

Chapter 2: Nelson Mandela's Tips On How To Customize Your Next Speech

Hopefully everyone knows who Nelson Mandela is – he's the South African leader **who's tireless efforts helped to get rid of his country's oppressive apartheid policies**. What is less known is how he marshaled world opinion in order to support the change that he wanted. It turns out that one way he made this happen was by giving speeches that uniquely connected with his audiences…

Nelson Mandela's Speeches

Nelson Madela spent 27 years in prison before he was released by the South African government. When he got out, **he quickly started to give speeches** that all had one common message: support his African National Congress (ANC) party in their attempt to create a new government.

It was important that Mandela work **his key message** into every speech that he gave. No matter where in the world he was, no matter who he was speaking to, his message was always the same: lend your support to the ANC.

This meant that he really had to give the same speech over and over again. However, he couldn't just show up and say the same thing each time – he would quickly lose the interest of his audiences. He needed to find a way to deliver his message in such a way that **it would appeal to his audience** while at the same time allowing him to incorporate his main message: please support the ANC.

It turns out the Nelson Mandela is a good speaker – he has a lot of natural ability. However, it was the realization that he needed to find ways to connect with his audience each time that he spoke that **turned him to a great speaker.**

How Nelson Mandela Connected With His Audience

Nelson Mandela connected with his audiences by taking the time to **customize the words that he was saying**. He knew that the core of each of his speeches needed to remain the same, support the ANC, but that he could modify the rest in order to reach out to and connect with the audience that he was addressing.

William Stevenson III has spent time studying the speeches that Mandela gave and he has been able to document the ways that the speeches were **customized for various audiences**.

When Mandela traveled to the United States, he gave a speech to a huge crowd in New York City's Harlem area. During this speech he changed it to include statements about how **his struggles in South Africa** were similar to the struggles of the Harlem residents to overcome their economic and social challenges.

Later in the same trip, Mandela addressed the U.S. Congress. During this speech he invoked the struggles that had been incorporated into the U.S. constitution and he related that to **what he was trying to accomplish in South Africa**.

What All Of This Means For You

Nelson Mandela is an accomplished political leader who successfully overthrew the oppressive apartheid policies that were holding his country back. One of the key skills that he used to do this was **his ability to deliver powerful speeches to diverse audiences**.

The only thing that the audiences that Mandela talked to had in common was that they were so very different. Mandela talked in multiple countries **always sharing the same message**: support my effort to cast out the current government of South Africa. In each country he would talk to different types of audiences. He would talk to common people in the street and leaders of government.

The way he was able to make his message connect with each of these audiences was by **customizing his words to match what was important to them**. He would use this type of tailored speech to capture the attention of his audience and then once they were connected, he would share his main message with them. We need to learn from Mandela and use his knowledge to reach our audiences so that our messages will make a lasting impression on them…

Chapter 3

How Speakers Can Help Other Speakers Be Their Best

Chapter 3: How Speakers Can Help Other Speakers Be Their Best

When we think about speaking in public, we normally think about one thing – ourselves. However, it turns out that that we really should be thinking bigger: **how can we help other speakers do better?** Since we know what it's like to stand in front of an audience and try to give a speech, we have a special obligation to use this knowledge to make the speeches that we attend become better speeches. Read on and find out what your new assignment is...

Keeping Calm When Nobody Else Is

As speakers we all know that there are **many things that can happen during a speech** that are out of control of the speaker. These can include such distractions as audience members' cell phones going off, fire alarms sounding, microphones that stop working, or any one of a number of different laptop related issues.

When you are the speaker and you have an event like this happen, **your stress level can start to go through the roof**. I mean you are already under a great deal of pressure to give a good speech, and now you have to deal with these additional challenges.

As speakers who are sitting in the audience, we can help a speaker get over these types of unplanned events simply by not reacting to them. Speakers feed off of the mood of their audience. When things start to go wrong, often times the audience will start to become restless or upset. When this happens, it's very easy for **the speaker to start to get upset also** – he or she is simply reflecting back to the audience the mood that they are picking up on.

When you are a member of the audience and these types of events start to happen, you can help out the speaker **by not getting upset**. Let your cool, calm demeanor influence the people sitting around you and help to keep them from becoming restless. The more people that you can influence this way, then the more positive energy will flow up to the speaker. This can significantly help them to stay on track and still give a good speech no matter what goes wrong for them!

Helping Out With The Old Q&A

No matter how clear a speaker is, **there will always be questions** that the audience has once the speaker is done talking. The audience may have thought up a question early on and has held it until the end of the speech, or perhaps based on their personal experiences they'd like to know how to apply what the speaker was talking about to their life.

The Q&A part of any speech can be a life & death proposition for any speaker. They complete their speech and then ask the audience if they have any questions. The sound of crickets that all too often greets them takes away from whatever they just got done talking about. As an audience, we tend to judge the quality of a speech by the quantity of questions that the speaker gets asked after they are done – more questions must mean that **the speech was a good speech**.

As speakers in the audience, this is a simple place for us to step in and **lend a helping hand to the presenter**. We need to listen very closely to the points that they are making in their speech. Then, when the Q&A portion of the speech is announced, we need to immediately raise our hand.

This **quick response** to the request for questions will minimize the amount of time that the speaker is "hanging" waiting for a question. Next, the question that we ask has to also help the speaker out.

We can make our question help the speaker by making sure that the question **reinforces their main point**. Questions that contain words like "If I understood your point correctly …" or "How could I apply that to my situation…" are great ways to do this.

Make sure that our question **keeps the speaker on track** and allows them to further expound on their main point even as they answer our question. The speaker will be forever grateful to you for allowing them to do this!

What All Of This Means For You

Giving a speech is never easy for anyone. As a speaker, since you know how hard it can be to give a good speech, you have **a special obligation** when you attend someone else's speech to do everything that you can to help their speech go well.

Since each speech is a unique performance, you can never be sure just exactly what is going to happen during the speech. That means that you're going to have to stay alert and **look for ways to help out**. One way that you can help is by keeping calm if things start to spin out of control during the speech. Another way to help is by being ready to ask good, topical questions if the speaker has a Q&A session.

I firmly believe that by helping out other speakers you can start to build a reputation as **a friend to all speakers**. When this happens, something magical will start to happen when you give a speech. Other speakers will be motivated to make sure that your speech goes well just like you have been doing for them. Do this often enough, you'll eventually have your entire audience working to help you deliver the best speech ever!

Chapter 4

Hey Speaker, What's Your Room IQ?

Chapter 4: Hey Speaker, What's Your Room IQ?

So how do you get ready to deliver a speech? Write out your words? Create some PowerPoint slides? It turns out that there's **one very important thing** that you may have been missing – taking control of the room that you'll be speaking in…

All The World's A Stage – Including Your Room

Sometimes when you give a speech, you actually do stand on a stage. However, other times you just stand in the front of a room. No matter how you do it, as the speaker **you get to define how large your "stage" is**.

The larger the room (and the audience) the larger you'll want your stage to be. This means that you'll use the left and right portions of the stage while you give your speech. If you're talking in a smaller room, or to a smaller audience, then you'll want to limit the amount of stage space that you are using in order to **boost the level of intimacy** that your audience feels.

As we've all seen when we've watched the really polished speakers, you never have to **just limit yourself to the front of the room**. If it works with your speech and if you are comfortable doing it, then you can walk to the back of the room while talking – as long as it works with what you are currently saying.

Finally, where your audience is sitting can be very important. We've all seen situations where the first few rows of a room are left empty by an audience that sat towards the back. As the speaker, you can invite (or insist that) your audience to fill in the front seats before you begin to speak.

How To Set Up Your Stage

One thing that you need to remember as a speaker: **you control the room**. Although there are sometimes limitations to what can be done, it never hurts to ask to have a room configured in the best way to match your speech.

One possible configuration is to have the chairs in the room **arranged in a circle**. This is a great way to make it easy for members of your audience to talk to each other. An alternative is to arrange the chairs in a "U" shape that allows eye contact and conversation between members of the audience while still keeping everyone's focus on you, the speaker.

As your audience becomes larger, your seating options become smaller. Generally for formal presentations, the standard classroom seating structure with rows and columns of seats works the best. When you are faced with this type of seating system, **you still have the ability to control the room**.

In order to take charge of a room, you need to be able to **take your speech to your audience**. This means that where you give your speech is up to you. You own the stage and you get to decide where you want to stand – and move to.

There is no one correct answer to the question of where a speaker should stand during a speech. Some prefer to remain at or close to the lectern, while others roam the entire stage. Pick which technique **works best for both you and your audience**.

Take Control Of Your Proximity

Your **physical distance from your audience** can be a key part of your speech. As the speaker, you control how much of a gap there is between you and the people that you are talking to.

The greater the distance, the more formal the speech will be interpreted as being. Since you have the ability to move around on the stage, you can reduce the amount of space between you and your audience no matter how big the room is. By reducing this space, you can make your speech **become more intimate** and connect more closely with your audience.

What All Of This Means For You

When you are giving a speech, you are in charge of everything and this includes the room in which you are delivering your speech. Taking the time to **set up the room in order to match your speech** is one of your most important tasks as a speaker.

When you are setting up the room that you'll be speaking in, **you can control where your audience sits** – are they far away from you, or are they up close? You can change the layout of the room based on the type of speech that you are giving – is it an intimate talk or is it a big presentation?

Speakers know that how they set up the room will determine **how close they can get to their audience**. If done correctly, then the room will help the speaker to make a positive lasting impression on the audience.

Chapter 5

Protect Your Next Speech From The Room!

Chapter 5: Protect Your Next Speech From The Room!

I'll bet that you didn't know that the next time that you give a speech, **the room is going to be actively conspiring against you!** Yep, it's true – no matter how cozy and inviting the room that you are going to be speaking in may appear, it is actually working against you. This room has chewed up and spit out tougher speakers than you – what makes you think that you'll do any better? The good news is that I know what you need to do in order to survive and I'm going to share it with you...

Why The Room Matters

Of all of the things that a speaker has to worry about when giving a speech, worrying about the room in which the speech will be given often comes towards the bottom of the list. However, it turns out that it should really be **much higher** on the list of things that we take care of...

The reason that the room can play such a large role in how your next speech is received is simply because **it is really a part of your speech**. If the room cooperates, then your audience will be comfortable and won't be distracted by outside noises. If the room doesn't cooperate, then it's going to be hard to pay attention to you because there will be plenty of other things going on that will distract your audience.

How To Make Peace With Your Room

Gene Perret is a professional speaker who has spent a lot of time studying how we can make peace with our rooms. He says that in order to be able to deliver an effective presentation, **speakers need to take control of their room**.

Remember, the room is **not just the physical space** that you'll occupy while you are giving your speech. Rather it's all that plus the things that are part of it: the sounds, the lights, the food that is being served, etc. You may not be able to control everything, but you can at least make sure that you know and understand the room that you'll be speaking in.

Perret believes that there are **3 things that we need to do as speakers** in order to make peace with our next room: know it, know your speech, and know how to make changes. Knowing the room is the most straight forward: how do you want the audience to be sitting – banquet, theater, or classroom seating? Will you be speaking from a stage or just standing at a head table?

The next step is to determine how your speech is going to **work with the room that you have**. What you are going to have to do is to adjust – you're going to have to make the speech that you are going to be giving work with the room that you have to work with. This can be as simple as standing on the middle of the stage so that everyone in a crowded room can see you or getting off the stage and walking in the audience if you have a smaller crowd.

Finally, you're going to have to be able to **adjust to the conditions that you find yourself with**. Sure you can change the things that can be changed before your audience shows up; however, there will probably be some things that you need to live with. As speakers we need to understand that this is the way that life goes and you need to make the best of the situation.

What All Of This Means For You

Every speaker needs to realize that the room in which they will be speaking will play **a key role** in how successful their next speech is. Ignore it at your own peril!

As a speaker you need to take charge of the room and **make it work with your speech, not against it**. This means arriving early so that you can become familiar with your room, understanding how your particular speech will (or won't) work with the room, and finally you need to know how to transform the room so that it will work with your speech.

Taking the time to understand the role that the room will play in your next speech is a technique that is used by the best speakers. If you follow their lead and make the room work with your speech, you'll be amazed at **just how friendly the room can become**.

Chapter 6

Bad Business News: A Speech That Speakers Need To Be Able To Give

Chapter 6: Bad Business News: A Speech That Speakers Need To Be Able To Give

Being asked to give a speech is a great honor. Being asked to give a speech that is going to deliver bad news to part or all of business is not such an honor. However, in order to be a truly good speaker, this is exactly the type of speech that you need to be able to step up and give. The keys are knowing how to organize this type of speech and what not to say…

How To Organize Bad News

When you've been asked to give bad news to people who work for a business, how you **organize the information** that you are going to be delivering is very important. Your audience is going to know why you are there so you are going to want to get to the main point of your speech as quickly as possible.

Kathy Berger has looked into how bad business news can be structured when it is delivered. She's come up with **four pillars** of information that always need to be included in this type of presentation:

Neutral Statement: Before you launch into delivering bad news to your audience, you'll want to take steps to get them to see the world the way that you currently see it. The best way to make this happen is to start your speech off with a neutral statement that everyone can agree with. This can be a simple observation of how things currently stand.

Bad News: Now is the time to deliver the bad news. You don't want to put this off because your audience is expecting and anticipating this news and if you delay giving it to them, then they won't be able to focus on anything else that you say until you do. You need to keep this very short – strip out all unnecessary words and simply focus on saying the bad thing that is going to happen.

Impact: Bad news is just bad news. What's really important to your audience is what this news means for them. If you don't tell them, they'll make it up on their own. This is why after you relay the bad news to them you need to quickly follow this up with clear statements that let your audience know how their world is going to change because of the bad news.

Details: When we receive bad news a 1,000 questions start to run through our minds. We're not happy and we want to see if perhaps some sort of mistake has been made, maybe something has been overlooked. That's why it is so important that you include the details that will provide answers to these questions in your speech. By tackling them in your speech, you improve the state of mind that your audience will end up leaving your speech in.

What Not To Do When You Are Delivering Bad News

So now that you know how to organize the bad business news that you are delivering, now we need to make sure that we know **what not to do** while delivering this information.

Don't lie. Although this seems like some basic advice, the desire to lie or even just stretch the truth a bit can be a powerful motivator when you are delivering bad news. Don't do it. Anytime that you try to tone down the bad news by saying something that is untrue it will always come back to bite you.

Don't be unclear. When what we have to say is difficult or painful to say, we often like to wrap it in a lot of words that we think will soften the blow. Don't do this. Your audience will have to work that much harder to understand what you are trying to say and they may even end up being confused.

Don't be insensitive. Bad business news will cause an emotional reaction in your audience. As a speaker you need to realize this and be tuned in to understanding how your audience is reacting to what you are saying. During this speech you are going to have to acknowledge this and show your audience that you understand how they are feeling.

Don't talk about you. In order to shield yourself from having to think about how this bad business news is going to be affecting your audience, we sometimes tend to make our speech all about us: how we feel about the news, what we are thinking, etc. Don't do this – your audience really doesn't care about you, they want to hear what all of this means for them.

What All Of This Means For You

Not all speeches are inspirational speeches – sometimes bad news has to be delivered. Giving this type of speech **is never easy** and that's why it's so important that we learn to do it the right way.

Organizing the speech correctly is **the first step** in effectively delivering bad news. Clearly telling your audience what the bad news is and then immediately following that up with words that will tell them what the impact of this information on them will be is the key to doing a good job. In this type of speech, how you say it can be as important as what you say. We've covered several things that you'll need to avoid.

Speakers who master the art of delivering bad business news will find that they have **become more valuable**. This type of speech will never be easy to give, but learn to do a good job of it and you'll always be in demand…

Chapter 7

What Harry Potter Can Teach You About Creating A Speech Introduction

Chapter 7: What Harry Potter Can Teach You About Creating A Speech Introduction

When you go to see a movie, what's the first thing that you always see? The answer is, of course, trailers! I must confess that there have been movies that I've gone to in the past in which the trailers were the best part of the whole movie viewing experience! What's interesting about these trailers is that they have been designed with one thing in mind: to get you to come back and see the movie that they are advertising. Maybe we can **learn something from trailers** that we can use in our next speech.

Why The Opening Of Your Speech Is So Very Important

Let's spend a moment thinking about **what runs through your mind** when you go to see a movie. You sit down in your seat, you've got your tub of popcorn, your gigantic cup of soda and you're in the mood to be entertained.

All of the ads and trailers get over and then the main feature starts. How long does it take you to figure out if you **are going to enjoy watching this movie?** How long is it before you might start thinking that the US$30 that you've spent to be sitting in this seat at this time was a big mistake? I'm willing to bet that this evaluation happens in less than a minute. Maybe even in less than 30 seconds.

Clearly, **how a movie starts** is a critical part of determining whether or not we're going to end up enjoying it. Sure, sure – sometimes a movie can start out badly and pull out a save in the end. However, these are rare occurrences – the opening pretty much determines what we're going to think about the whole movie.

Although you and I are not in the movie making business, we do spend our time **making and delivering speeches**. If you're willing to come a long with me for just a moment or two, then I'd like to propose that a speech is very much like a movie. We know about the importance of public speaking and it's up to us to show our audience how important what we have to say is. We've got an audience and we'd like to capture their attention (no matter how good their listening skills are) and hold it throughout our entire speech. Hmm, I wonder just how we can go about doing this...

How To Build A Speech Opening That's Like A Movie Trailer

Maybe we should take an easier route here. Instead of trying to worry about building our entire speech like a movie, let's just focus for now on **building our speech's opening like a movie trailer**.

What is the purpose of a movie trailer? It's a quick 1-2 minute video presentation that is designed to **get us interested** enough in an upcoming movie that we'll come back to the movie theater and pay to see it. Hmm, this attention grabbing thing sounds exactly like what we try to do when we are starting our speech.

How does a movie trailer work its magic on us? It's actually pretty simple. A movie trailer has to **immediately grab our attention**. No matter if it's an explosion, a gunshot, or a face slap, it has very little time so it has to move quickly.

The next thing that has to happen in a movie trailer is that we need to be **introduced to the characters**. This needs to happen fast and we need to understand who they are and what they are trying to do. They may be an archeologist, a superhero, a wizard, it doesn't matter – the background is being set up. This also needs to be done quickly.

A movie trailer only has time to accomplish one more thing. The people that we've just been introduced to now have to be put into some sort of **challenging situation** that there appears to be no way for them to get out of. This is the "hook" that will make us come back to the movie theater in order to find out how things turn out.

When you are creating the opening for your next speech, you are going to want to do the same set of steps. You have **very little time in which to capture your audience's attention** and so you're going to have move quickly. The first words out of your mouth are going to have to grab their attention. You're going to have to follow this up with a description of the situation that you'll be talking about and the people who will be involved. Finally, you'll need to create a challenging situation to end your introduction. This challenge is what's going to cause your audience to remain sitting in their seats and listening to your entire speech.

What All Of This Means For You

The first few words that tumble out of your mouth during your next speech **set the stage** for the rest of the speech that is to follow. One of the benefits of public speaking is that you control what you say and so you can create a powerful introduction for your next speech. Your speech's introduction is a critical part of making the entire speech effective.

In order to design a speech opening that will both grab and hold your audience's attention, **take a look at how movie trailers do it**. They always open with a bang – they grab your attention. Next, they introduce the characters and provide some background info, and finally they place them in some sort of situation that appears to be difficult / impossible to get out of.

This is exactly what you need to do in your speech's opening in order to hook your audience. Forget all of those presentation tips – the opening of your speech is where it's at.

The opening of your speech is only one part of the total speech. However, if you get this part correct, then the rest of the speech will be **much easier to do correctly**. Take the time to craft a great "trailer" for your next speech and your audience will end up giving you a great review!

Chapter 8

---

5 Ways For Public Speakers To Not Say "I'm Sorry"

Chapter 8: 5 Ways For Public Speakers To Not Say "I'm Sorry"

Oh, oh – now you've done it. Somehow, in some way, you screwed up. You made a mistake and did something (or in many cases you said something) that was wrong. What are you going to do now? The best thing to do would be to apologize and hope that your audience is using their listening skills. However, it turns out that this is just a bit more difficult than it seems...

The Problem With Saying "I'm Sorry"

So why do we even bother with saying "I'm sorry" in the first place? When we do something wrong, we offend others. This means that they are going to be less willing to work with us and to help us out. If we go to the effort of apologizing, then we can mend fences with these people and get things back to the way that they used to be.

One-on-one apologies are fairly simple to do. However, when we've done something that has offended a larger group of people, then that's when our public speaking skills are going to have to come into play and the true importance of public speaking is going to have to save the day.

5 Ways To Not Say "I'm Sorry"

Just as there are many ways to correctly tell the world that you regret what you've done, there are just as many ways to do a bad job of it. No presentation tips are going to help you out here. The author Chris Witt has taken a look into how we can make up for the wrongs that we've done. Let's take a look at 5 ways that you should not go about saying "I'm Sorry".

Duck!: As kids we all did this – when we were caught doing something wrong we were quick to blame someone else: "He did it!" As speakers, we can't do this. We need to "man up" and take responsibility for our own actions.

Hide: It's not your fault if there were a set of circumstances that ended up forcing you to do or say what you did. This is another classic defense that won't go over very well with your audience. Don't even try it. Instead, accept responsibility no matter what the sequence of events was that led you to where you were.

Others Did It: This is an interesting defense that your audience might not pick up on for a while, but they'll see through it eventually. When you use the passive voice to offer your apology you deflect the blame on to others by talking about what happened in an onlooker way: "Facts were incorrectly evaluated and a bad decision was made". You made the bad decision, tell everyone that you are sorry that you made it.

Time Is On Your Side: Every event has a timeline associated with it. This means that from the moment that the mistake is made going forward, things can happen or not. When you choose to make an apology is important. You may be tempted to wait as long as possible in the hopes that the whole thing will blow over. Don't. The sooner that you apologize, the quicker the event will become defused.

Keep It All Inside: Making a mistake and then having to apologize is a big deal for all of us who are not emotionless serial killers. This means that while you are making your apology, there is a good chance that some of your emotions will come spilling out around the edges. This is a good thing – it shows that you are human. Don't let your emotions obscure your message, but do let them show.

What All Of This Means For You

We all make mistakes. Even knowing this, we will all continue to make mistakes. What this means is that we need to become good at asking for forgiveness. The ability to say "I'm sorry" and to be believed is the key to starting to move beyond whatever we've done.

As easy as this may appear to be able to do, it turns out that it's quite difficult to do it well. One of the benefits of public speaking is that we can apologize to a large group of people all at the same time. Speakers need to be careful to avoid making the 5 mistakes that we've discussed when offering an apology.

Learning to make a good apology may be something that none of us instinctively wants to do; however, the benefits can be substantial. When people believe that you mean what you are saying then you'll be able to quickly move beyond the situation that you find yourself in. This is a skill that is well worth developing.

Chapter 9

The Value Of Time – What A Public Speaker Needs To Know

Chapter 9: The Value Of Time – What A Public Speaker Needs To Know

How long should your next speech be? Or maybe the more important question is, how long is too long? When we are asked to give a speech, there is an implied amount of time that we are being asked to fill. We are generally part of a bigger program and this is why **time is so important**: you need to know how to use your time in the right way...

How You See Time

I speak from experience when I say that how I see time as a speaker is probably very different from how the event planner that has set up my speaking opportunity sees it. We all know about the importance of public speaking and to do my part I know that I have a specific amount of information that I want to communicate to my audience. I'm going to accomplish that in my speech. The trick is to figure out **how much time I'll have in which to do it!**

Often times I find myself as part of **a program of speakers**. This means that time has all of sudden become even more important. Not only do I need to be careful and use up only the time that has been allocated to me, but my fellow speakers had better do the same.

This means that I always take the time to ask **how long I'm going to have to give my speech**. Trust me, this information is more important than any presentation tips that you might be given. I'm also careful to ask once again when I arrive where I'll be giving the speech. I can't tell you how many times I've been told that my speaking time has shrunk due to issues that have popped up.

Keep in mind that when you are actually speaking, there is a trick to **wining the favor of your audience**. In order to win the eternal gratitude of your audience, all you have to do is to finish just a little bit early. Keep in mind that they'll be upset with you if you screw up and finish just a little bit late!

How They See Time

The person who invited you to give a speech sees time completely differently than you do. Whereas you just see the time that has been allocated to your speech, they see the time that the event is going to be taking up as a whole. Your speech is just a small part of **something much larger**.

This means that when you find yourself playing the role of event planner, you need to **change how you view time**. As you arrange for speakers to participate in your event, you need to make sure that you clearly communicate to them how long you want them to talk for. Don't allow there to be any confusion!

Speakers are **notoriously fickle** when it comes to making commitments and then following through. As an event organizer, you are going to need to make sure that you reach out and confirm their participation in your event roughly a week before you need to have them show up.

Speakers struggle to keep track of time while they are speaking. This means that as the event planner you are going to be in charge of making sure that **they know how much time they've used up**. This can be done via hand signals or the holding up of signs from the back of the room. Make sure that they know how much time they have before they have to wrap things up.

Finally, as the event organizer you are **the ultimate decider** of when a presentation is over. If a speaker is not wrapping up and it's time to move on to the next presenter, then you're going to have to step in (yes, I know that it's rude) and thank the speaker and then tell everyone that it's time for the next speaker to take the stage.

What All Of This Means For You

No matter what role you are playing in your next speaking event, speaker or planner, you need to make sure that **you have a firm grasp of time**. If you don't make the effort to control time, then you'll be doing your audience a great disservice – no matter how good their listening skills are.

As a speaker it is your job to maximize the benefits of public speaking. To do this, you need to find out **how much time has been allocated for your speech**. If no time limit has been set, then you need to both set one and stick to it. As a planner you need to tell each speaker how much time they have to deliver their speech. You then need to manage each speech and ensure that the speaker wraps things up on time.

Time is the most precious thing that both a speaker and an audience have. When you give a speech or arrange for speeches to be given, you need to take the time to make sure that **only the time that has been allocated will be used**. Remember, if you can end things early, your audience will love you forever!

Chapter 10

Hello – Just Exactly Who Are You?

Chapter 10: Hello – Just Exactly Who Are You?

Got any thoughts on how you would like to start your next speech? What words of wisdom will you use to start your speech in a way that will capture the hearts and minds of your audience from the get-go and cause them to use their listening skills to really hear what you have to say? Hold on, it turns out that if you wait until you start speaking to start your speech **you may already be too late** — no presentation tips are going to save you now. I've got a better way for you to get your next speech off to a good start...

How An Introduction Is Supposed To Work

So why do speakers go to the effort to get someone to introduce them? Doesn't the audience already know who they are – I mean after all, **the audience has shown up** and they all know about the importance of public speaking, right?

It turns out that there's a very good chance that **your audience does not know who you are**. They may have come because of the topic that you'll be talking about; however, they may know nothing about you.

That's why you always want to coordinate with the person who is running the event in order to get them to agree to provide you with an introduction. Your introduction is going to serve you in **two different ways**.

First, it's going to make sure that **your audience knows who you are**. You are planning on standing up in front of your audience and talking for the next 30-60-90 minutes, why should they bother to listen to you? The introduction that is delivered about you should tell your audience why they are lucky to have an opportunity to hear you.

Next, your introduction can **set the stage for your speech**. Without going into too much detail, the introduction can touch on what you'll be talking about. It's often best to ask your introducer to tease the audience with what questions you'll be answering during your speech and not focus on the points that you'll be covering.

Preparing For The Worst

Considering how important an introduction is to your next speech, it sure seems as though it would be a good idea to take steps to **ensure that it goes well**. What this means is that you need to prepare for the worst to happen.

The most important step in your **"introduction defense system"** needs to be that you always remember to bring a hardcopy of the introduction that you've created for this speech to the speech itself. There are actually a couple of different reasons for doing this.

The first is that in this crazy mixed up world that we live in, there is always a good chance that the person who is going to be introducing you just might **misplace the introduction that you gave to them**. If this happens, all too often the person may be too proud to admit it and then may try to wing your introduction with disastrous results. Always have a backup hardcopy for them to use.

Secondly, the person who had agreed to provide you with an introduction **may not even be at the event!** Things can happen and schedules can change. There's nothing that we can do to prevent this from happening; however, if you have a copy of your introduction then you can quickly hand it to the replacement introducer and you should be good to go.

What All Of This Means For You

It can be a bit frightening as a speaker to realize that how your next speech is going to turn out may be determined **even before you have a chance to open your mouth**. The good news is that once you know this, you can take action to make sure that everything starts off on a good foot.

Before you start to give your next speech, **make sure that someone is going to introduce you**. If you've set up with someone to be introduced and for whatever reason they can't do it, make sure that you've come prepared to have someone else step in and take care of it.

Introductions set the tone for a speech and the fact that we get to use an introduction is one of the benefits of public speaking. Even before you start to say anything, your introduction can set the tone for your speech and may determine its outcome. Do your homework and make sure that your next speech comes with a great introduction!

Chapter 11

Talking Business: Tips For Speaker Success

Chapter 11: Talking Business: Tips For Speaker Success

Giving a speech in a business environment, specifically **to a group of senior managers**, can be one of the most difficult speeches that any of us will ever be called on to give. However, even this type of speech can be done smoothly and will allow you to be seen as an effective communicator if only you take the time to follow the following suggestions.

Talk About The Downside Of Your Proposal

One of the things that speakers seem to forget is that our audiences are made up of bright, smart people. What this means for you is that even as you are speaking, they are going to be **mentally racing ahead of you**.

What this means is that they are going to be **picking apart** what you are talking about and they'll be realizing that there are costs and drawbacks to what you are discussing or proposing. If you don't touch on these issues, then you'll be leaving some very big unanswered questions in the minds of your audience when you are done talking.

The best way to deal with this issue is head on – **discuss the downside of your proposal**. However, since you are the one who is bringing it up, you get to control how it gets discussed. This means that you can discuss it in the most positive way possible. One clever way to go about doing this is to focus on just how expensive it would be for your audience to not take your advice or to not follow your plan. This might serve two purposes: you'll deal with the downside of your proposal and you'll convince your audience to accept your proposal.

Be Very, Very Specific

When you are dealing with a business audience, one of your biggest challenges will be to **keep their attention**. You are probably addressing them in an office environment and there are a number of other activities that will be competing with you for their attention (like smartphones).

What this means is that you need to make the effort to **keep focused** during your presentation – you are going to want to be very, very specific about what you are talking about. You want to make sure that at no time does your audience have to work to understand specifically what you are getting at.

This also means that no matter how tempting it may be, you need to **be sure to not wander off subject**. At the same time you need to make sure that you don't start to talk in generalities – keep your presentation sharp and on target.

What All Of This Means For You

Making a business presentation to a group of senior managers can be both a nerve racking and **a career limiting event**. You can do this successfully; however, in order to be successful you need to do the right things and not do the wrong things.

You need to realize that your audience is going to be thinking about what you are saying and they will be able to **quickly identify any downsides or costs** associated with your presentation. Make sure that you deal with these issues right off the bat and do so in the most positive way possible. As you make your presentation, be as specific as possible – stay on target and be sure to not wander.

The ultimate goal of any speech that we give is to **change the world** in some way. Giving a business presentation to senior management allows us to make this happen if we take the time to do it correctly.

Chapter 12

2 Tips For Giving A Successful Business Speech

Chapter 12: 2 Tips For Giving A Successful Business Speech

Giving a speech in a business environment, specifically **to a group of senior managers**, can be one of the most difficult speeches that any of us will ever be called on to give. However, even this type of speech can be done smoothly and will allow you to be seen as an effective communicator if only you take the time to follow the following suggestions.

What You Looking At?

There are many differences between the speeches that we give in "the real world" and the ones that we'll deliver in a business setting. However, there is one thing that both of these types of speeches have in common: **we need to use our eyes correctly**.

What this means is that we need to remember that both ourselves and our audiences are human beings. Because of this, we both send and receive a great deal of communication when we are talking by using our eyes. If we don't do this correctly, then our message is going to come across as being **garbled and confused**.

Due to the fact that delivering any speech in a business setting can be a high pressure undertaking, it is perfectly natural for the speaker to **not want to make eye contact** with his or her audience. Instead, we'd prefer to focus on our notes or our slides so that we can make sure that we're getting our words to come out correctly.

You need to be very careful to not do this. **Take the time to look everyone in the room in the eye while you deliver your speech**. It's only by doing this that you'll be able to come across as being honest and believable. The idea that you are presenting will be much better received if you are able to connect with your audience by making eye contact with each and every one of them during your speech.

Short Is Good In A Business Presentation

The one thing that your audience does not have enough of is time. We are all **starved for time** these days and so the simple fact that your audience took the time out of their day to show up for your presentation should be taken as a compliment to you.

Once you have them sitting before you, you then need to treat their time as **the valuable thing that it is**. The presentation that you give needs to be as short as you can make it.

The trick here is to make sure that you **completely cover all of the required information** while at the same time using as few words as is possible. I must confess to wanting to include everything that I know into a speech so that my audience will walk away knowing as much as I do about a topic. You must resist this.

Instead, think about what you want your audience to be able to remember and to repeat after your presentation. Once you know this, then you'll know what needs to be included in your speech – and what you can leave out!

What All Of This Means For You

Making a business presentation to a group of senior managers can be both a nerve racking and **a career limiting event**. You can do this successfully; however, in order to be successful you need to do the right things and not do the wrong things.

The goal of any business speech is to make contact with your audience and to get them to agree with your idea and perhaps approve your proposal. In order to make this happen, you need to take the time to make eye contact during your speech with everyone in the room. You'll also have to respect the value of their time and work to keep your presentation as short as possible.

The ultimate goal of any speech that we give is to **change the world** in some way. Giving a business presentation to senior management allows us to make this happen if we take the time to do it correctly.

It's from the forge of failure that the steel of success is formed.

Hard Work Does Not Guarantee Success, But Success Does Not Happen Without Hard Work.

- Dr. Jim Anderson

Create Speeches That Motivate Your Audiences And Get Your Message Heard!

Dr. Jim Anderson is available to provide training and coaching on the topics that are the most important to people who have to speak in public: how can I create a speech that people want to hear and how can I deliver in a way that will allow me to connect with my audience and get my point across to them?

Dr. Anderson believes that in order to both learn and remember what he says, speakers need to laugh. Each one of his speeches is full of fun and humor so that what he says "sticks" with everyone.

Dr. Anderson's Public Speaking Training Includes:

1. How to plan your next speech: pick your purpose and understand your audience.
2. What's the best way to get PowerPoint and Keynote to work with you, not against you?
3. What do you need to do when you are presenting in order to truly connect with your audience?

Dr. Jim Anderson presents over 100 speeches per year. To invite Dr. Anderson to speak at your event, contact him at:

Phone: 813-418-6970 or
Email: jim@BlueElephantConsulting.com

65

Photo Credits:

Cover – Celine Nadeau
https://www.flickr.com/photos/celinet/

Chapter 1 – jj.sheets
https://www.flickr.com/photos/11249990@N06/

Chapter 2 - lasanta.com.ec
https://www.flickr.com/photos/45582474@N02/

Chapter 3 - Paul Swansen
https://www.flickr.com/photos/pswansen/

Chapter 4 - UAF School of Management
https://www.flickr.com/photos/uafsom/

Chapter 5 - Kena Siu
https://www.flickr.com/photos/makkens/

Chapter 6 - Jessica Crabtree
https://www.flickr.com/photos/jessicacrabtree/

Chapter 7 - Carol Smith
https://www.flickr.com/photos/clsphotos/

Chapter 8 – LexnGer
https://www.flickr.com/photos/lexnger/

Chapter 9 - kitchener.lord
https://www.flickr.com/photos/27862259@N02/

Chapter 10 - DFID - UK Department for International Development
https://www.flickr.com/photos/dfid/

Chapter 11 - Army Medicine
https://www.flickr.com/photos/armymedicine/

Chapter 12 - Allan LEONARD
https://www.flickr.com/photos/mrulster/

Other Books By The Author

Product Management

- How Product Managers Can Sell More Of Their Product: Tips & Techniques For Product Managers To Better Understand How To Sell Their Product

- How Product Managers Can Sell More Of Their Product: Tips & Techniques For Product Managers To Better Understand How To Sell Their Product

- How To Create A Successful Product That Customers Will Want: Techniques For Product Managers To Boost Product Sales And Increase Customer Satisfaction

- What Product Managers Need To Know About World-Class Product Development: How Product Managers Can Create Successful Products

- How Product Managers Can Learn To Understand Their Customers: Techniques For Product Managers To Better Understand What Their Customers Really Want

- Product Management Secrets: Techniques For Product Managers To Boost Produ Michael Kct Sales And Increase Customer Satisfaction

- Product Development Lessons For Product Managers: How Product Managers Can Create Successful Products

- Customer Lessons For Product Managers: Techniques For Product Managers To Better Understand What Their Customers Really Want

- Product Failure Lessons For Product Managers: Examples Of Products That Have Failed For Product Managers To Learn From

- Communication Skills For Product Managers: The Communication Skills That Product Managers Need To Know How To Use In Order To Have A Successful Product

- How To Have A Successful Product Manager Career: The Things That You Need To Be Doing TODAY In Order To Have A Successful Product Manager Career

- Product Manager Product Success: How to keep your product on track and make it become a success

Public Speaking

- Changing How You Speak To Overcome Your Fear Of Speaking: Change techniques that will transform a speech into a memorable event

- Delivering Excellence: How To Give Presentations That Make A Difference: Presentation techniques that will transform a speech into a memorable event

- Tools Speakers Need In Order To Give The Perfect Speech: What tools to use to create your next speech so that your message will be remembered forever!

- How To Create A Speech That Will Be Remembered

- Secrets To Organizing A Speech For Maximum Impact: How to put together a speech that will capture and hold your audience's attention

- How To Become A Better Speaker By Changing How You Speak: Change techniques that will transform a speech into a memorable event

- How To Give A Great Presentation: Presentation techniques that will transform a speech into a memorable event

- How To Rehearse In Order To Give The Perfect Speech: How to effectively rehearse your next speech to that your message be remembered forever!

- Secrets To Creating The Perfect Speech: How to create a speech that will make your message be remembered forever!

- Secrets To Organizing The Perfect Speech: How to organize the best speech of your life!

- Secrets To Planning The Perfect Speech: How to plan to give the best speech of your life

- How To Show What You Mean During A Presentation: How to use visual techniques to transform a speech into a memorable event

CIO Skills

- Keeping The Barbarians Out: How CIOs Can Secure Their Department and Company: Tips And Techniques For CIOs To Use In Order To Secure Both Their IT Department And Their Company

- What CIOs Need To Know In Order To Successfully Manage An IT Department: Decision Making Skills That Every CIO Needs To Have In Order To Be Able

To Make The Right Choices

- Becoming A Powerful And Effective Leader: Tips And Techniques That IT Managers Can Use In Order To Develop Leadership Skills

- CIO Secrets For Growing Innovation: Tips And Techniques For CIOs To Use In Order To Make Innovation Happen In Their IT Department

- Your Success As A CIO Depends On How Well You Communicate: Tips And Techniques For CIOs To Use In Order To Become Better Communicators

- What CIOs Need To Know About Working With Partners: Techniques For CIOs To Use In Order To Be Able To Successfully Work With Partners

- Critical CIO Management Skills: Decision Making Skills That Every CIO Needs To Have In Order To Be Able To Make The Right Choices

- How CIOs Can Make Innovation Happen: Tips And Techniques For CIOs To Use In Order To Make Innovation Happen In Their IT Department

- CIO Communication Skills Secrets: Tips And Techniques For CIOs To Use In Order To Become

Better Communicators

- Managing Your CIO Career: Steps That CIOs Have To Take In Order To Have A Long And Successful Career

- CIO Business Skills: How CIOs can work effectively with the rest of the company!

IT Manager Skills

- How To Build High Performance IT Teams: Tips And Techniques That IT Managers Can Use In Order To Develop Productive Teams

- Save Yourself, Save Your Job – How To Manage Your IT Career: Secrets That IT Managers Can Use In Order To Have A Successful Career

- Growing Your CIO Career: How CIOs Can Work With The Entire Company In Order To Be Successful

- How IT Managers Can Make Innovation Happen: Tips And Techniques For IT Managers To Use In Order To Make Innovation Happen In Their Teams

- Staffing Skills IT Managers Must Have: Tips And Techniques That IT Managers Can Use In Order To

Correctly Staff Their Teams

- Secrets Of Effective Leadership For IT Managers: Tips And Techniques That IT Managers Can Use In Order To Develop Leadership Skills

- IT Manager Career Secrets: Tips And Techniques That IT Managers Can Use In Order To Have A Successful Career

- IT Manager Budgeting Skills: How IT Managers Can Request, Manage, Use, And Track Their Funding

- Secrets Of Managing Budgets: What IT Managers Need To Know In Order To Understand How Their Company Uses Money

Negotiating

- Exploring How To Get The Deal That You Want In A Negotiation: How To Develop The Skill Of Exploring What Is Possible In A Negotiation In Order To Reach The Best Possible Deal

- Use The Power Of Arguing To Win Your Next Negotiation: How To Develop The Skill Of Effective Arguing In A Negotiation In Order To Get The Best Possible Outcome

- Learn How To Signal In Your Next Negotiation: How To Develop The Skill Of Effective Signaling In A Negotiation In Order To Get The Best Possible Outcome

- Learn The Skill Of Exploring In A Negotiation: How To Develop The Skill Of Exploring What Is Possible In A Negotiation In Order To Reach The Best Possible Deal

- Learn How To Argue In Your Next Negotiation: How To Develop The Skill Of Effective Arguing In A Negotiation In Order To Get The Best Possible Outcome|

- How To Open Your Next Negotiation: How To Start A Negotiation In Order To Get The Best Possible Outcome

- Preparing For Your Next Negotiation: What You Need To Do BEFORE A Negotiation Starts In Order To Get The Best Possible Deal

- Learn How To Package Trades In Your Next Negotiation

- All Good Things Come To An End: How To Close A Negotiation - How To Develop The Skill Of Closing In Order To Get The Best Possible Outcome From A

Negotiation

- Take No Prisoners In Your Next Negotiation: How To Start A Negotiation In Order To Get The Best Possible Outcome

Miscellaneous

- How To Heal A Broken Leg – Fast!: Understanding how to deal with a broken leg in order to start walking again quickly

- How Software Defined Networking (SDN) Is Going To Change Your World Forever: The Revolution In Network Design And How It Affects You

- The Power Of Virtualization: How It Affects Memory, Servers, and Storage: The Revolution In Creating Virtual Devices And How It Affects You

- The Internet-Enabled Successful School District Superintendent: How To Use The Internet To Boost Parental Involvement In Your Schools

- Power Distribution Unit (PDU) Secrets: What Everyone Who Works In A Data Center Needs To Know!

- Making The Jump: How To Land Your Dream Job When You Get Out Of College!

- How To Use The Internet To Create Successful Students And Involved Parents

"How to put together a speech that will capture and hold your audience's attention"

This book has been written with one goal in mind – to show you how you can organize a powerful and effective speech We're going to show you how to make sure that your next speech clearly communicates your message!

Let's Make Your Next Speech A Success!

What You'll Find Inside:

- SPEAKERS NEED TO KNOW WHAT THEIR EMOTIONAL INTELLIGENCE QUOTIENT IS

- NELSON MANDELA'S TIPS ON HOW TO CUSTOMIZE YOUR NEXT SPEECH

- HEY SPEAKER, WHAT'S YOUR ROOM IQ?

- WHAT HARRY POTTER CAN TEACH YOU ABOUT CREATING A SPEECH INTRODUCTION

Dr. Jim Anderson brings his 25 years of real-world experience to this book. He's delivered speeches at some of the world's largest firms as well as at many conferences. He's going to show you what you need to do in order to make your next speech a success!

www.ingramcontent.com/pod-product-compliance
Lightning Source LLC
Chambersburg PA
CBHW061159180526
45170CB00002B/878